101
THINGS THAT
PISS ME OFF

101

THINGS THAT
PISS ME OFF

RACHEL BALLINGER

ST. MARTIN'S GRIFFIN ☙ NEW YORK

www.stmartins.com

Designed by Anna Gorovoy

The Library of Congress Cataloging-in-Publication Data
is available upon request.

ISBN 978-1-250-12930-7 (paper over board)
ISBN 978-1-250-12931-4 (e-book)

Our books may be purchased in bulk for promotional, educational,
or business use. Please contact your local bookseller or the Macmillan
Corporate and Premium Sales Department at 1-800-221-7945, extension
5442, or by e-mail at MacmillanSpecialMarkets@macmillan.com.

First Edition: June 2017

10   9   8   7   6   5   4   3   2   1

Introduction

Have you ever gotten so angry that your fists curled, all of your muscles tightened, and every word out of your mouth was a scream? Then someone tells you to "calm down" because it's "not that big of a deal"? Screw that person! I hate that person! You have the right to be unnecessarily angry. You have the right to curse, scream, and throw things. Most people might not get angry at someone for going the speed limit. But lucky for you, I'm not most people. I will yell at that law-abiding citizen. I will scream at them (from the safety of my car) and tell them how stupid I think they are. Because that person Pissed. Me. Off. My name is Rachel Ballinger, and I have (admittedly, to a fault) a short and loud temper.

Welcome to my list of 101 things that piss me off. Some of these things are serious. Some of these things are petty. Some of them might be considered "first world problems." However, I call them annoyances that simply need to stop. And I feel that most of you will agree with me (but frankly, I do not care if you do or don't). Let's do this.

THINGS PEOPLE DO

—

YOU KNOW WHAT PISSES ME OFF??

When people ask me "Does this smell weird?"

Never. Never do I ever want to be your sniff tester.
Why would I? Chances are, it does smell weird! If
you are questioning the smell of something, it usually means the smell is questionable. Don't put it
near me. Ya nasty.

Also, don't ask me to taste anything, either. . . . My
friend once asked me to taste her milk for her, and I
ended up spraying white chunky liquid all over the
kitchen and shoving anything I could find into my
mouth to get rid of the sour taste!

Have some human decency; if something smells
questionable, just throw it out.

When people say water doesn't have a taste.

You're wrong. It does. It tastes like water. End of story.

YOU KNOW WHAT PISSES ME OFF??

When people type *haha* or *LOL*.

Now, I'm not against these things. They express laughter or that something was funny. I often write them to express such things. But let's be real, when people type *haha* or *LOL,* you know that zero laughter came from their body. So unless you write: *BAHAHAHAHAKHFDKHAHAHAHAH,* I won't think you actually found anything funny.

And adding an *LOL* at the end of an uncomfortable text doesn't make it less uncomfortable. In fact, it makes it more uncomfortable.

Here's an example of an *LOL* not helping:

That *LOL* just made everything 80x more awkward!

4

YOU KNOW WHAT PISSES ME OFF??

How people get 10x stupider when entering an airport or airplane.

People forget how to walk, buckle a seat belt, follow a sign, follow verbal instructions, push a button, or even how to carry a bag once they've stepped into an airport, especially in the security line. It really isn't that hard to figure out that you have to take off your shoes, belt, and jacket, then take out your laptop. Also, don't bring objects that can kill people or any large containers full of mysterious liquid. These are very simple rules. And then once you're through the scanning process, please step aside while you redress yourself so the rest of us can get to our bags. It's not rocket science, people.

5

YOU KNOW WHAT PISSES ME OFF??

When people don't brush their teeth immediately after waking up.

When I wake up, my mouth tastes disgusting. Everybody's does. How can people get out of bed and think, "Yes! This is the taste I want in my mouth the rest of the morning"? It's gross. Brush your teeth. And don't use the excuse, "Well, I want to eat breakfast first." Here's a bit of information, you can eat breakfast after you brush your teeth. I know, I just blew your mind. You're welcome.

6
YOU KNOW WHAT PISSES ME OFF??

When people roll down my window in the car without asking.

I'm a human with long hair that, on most days, I wear down. That means that if a lot of wind blows in my face, my hair blows everywhere and gets completely tangled, resulting in me hating everything the rest of the day. People with short hair don't understand this problem; therefore, it's usually short-haired people who decide to roll down my window without asking and get so confused when I roll it back up or threaten to murder them. This is just a warning to every human out there: people with long hair usually don't like it blowing in their face. Keep the windows up. You can roll down yours all you want . . . but you better not let that wind touch my hair.

Window down:

Window up:

7
YOU KNOW WHAT PISSES ME OFF??

When you text someone something really funny and then they don't respond.

Excuse me. . . . That was funny, write back.

8
YOU KNOW WHAT PISSES ME OFF??

When people start a sentence with "I'm sorry, but ..."

Chances are, they're not sorry. My father taught me that a true apology should never have "but" in it. If you are trying to excuse your actions, then you are not taking full responsibility for them. Or if you say, "I'm sorry, but ..." before you actually do the thing that you're apologizing for, then you're not sorry in the least bit. Because if you were sorry, you wouldn't have done it in the first place.

It's the same as saying, "I'm sorry you feel that way." That's not an apology.

I see you fake apologizing. I see you.

I've made a list of fake apologies and excuses, so that you can look out for them. Or so you stop using them....

1. "I'm sorry, but I'm the kind of person that always tells the truth, so I had to tell that guy you liked him."
2. "I'm sorry, but you're dumb if you thought that test was hard."
3. "I'm sorry, but I was just really hungry, so I had to eat your lunch or I would have gotten really cranky."
4. "Sorry that I have to say this, but you look fat in that."
5. "I'm sorry that I told everyone your biggest secret, but you were being annoying earlier so I had every right."

Those aren't real apologies or excuses.

9

YOU KNOW WHAT PISSES ME OFF??

When store employees are up my butt the entire time I'm in the store.

I know most retail salespeople work on commission. Therefore, they are friendly, ask if I need help, and try to do whatever they can to make my shopping experience as blissful as possible. . . . But for me that means letting me shop in peace and not reminding me of your sales promotion 6 times, asking if I need something in a different size, if I need help finding something, what I'm looking for that day, what my favorite color is, what I ate that day, what my favorite season is, where I'm from, if I like cats or dogs better, which Kardashian I'm most like, and then telling me about your sales promotion once more. I'm a grown competent woman. I can read your sale signs, and I know that if I have any problems, you'll be there to help me. You don't need to hold my hand. I know I sound like a terrible person right now. . . . It's because I am. But on the real, leave me alone. A cordial, "Hello, need help with anything today?" is fine.

10
YOU KNOW WHAT PISSES ME OFF??

When people say "no offense."

That does not make things any less offensive. You know it's offensive and yet you say it anyway. If you are about to say something offensive, instead of saying, "no offense," just don't say the offensive thing. That seems like a better idea. If you do say something offensive, you're stupid. No offense, though.

11

When people chew with their mouths open.

If someone is smacking their lips and chewing with their mouth open, I actually get violent and will leave the town they are in. It's happened before. Just ask anyone in my family.

It's all about the sound. I can't stand the wet smacking sound. It's an actual disorder called *misophonia*. I don't get how everyone doesn't have this disorder when they hear this particular sound, though. How do people think it's okay to chew like that? Do they like to test the law of gravity and see how far open they can get their mouth without the food falling out? Here are diagrams of how a mouth should and shouldn't look when eating:

How it should look:

How it shouldn't look:

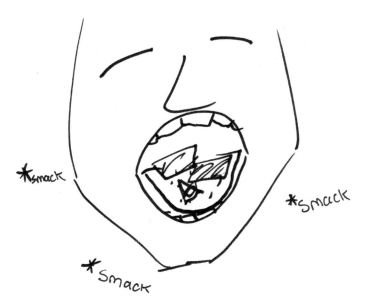

*smack

*smack

*smack

So if you ever want to have a meal with me and not have your face bashed against the table, chew with your mouth closed and don't make wet smacking noises when you take a bite.

12
YOU KNOW WHAT PISSES ME OFF??

When people miss a high five on purpose.

SCREW YOU! Hitting a perfect high five is a ridiculously satisfying feeling. Missing a high five is the worst feeling ever. When someone does it on purpose, i.e., "down low, too slow," that makes them a disgusting person who should rot in hell. How dare you. How dare you take away an amazing feeling and replace it with a terrible one. I hate you. You're not funny. You're mean and make my heart sad.

Side note: If you're terrible at high fives, look at the person's elbow and not their hand. You'll never miss. :)

13

YOU KNOW WHAT PISSES ME OFF??

When people take "Snowy Mirror Pictures."

When someone takes a picture of themselves in a mirror, but that mirror is so dirty that it looks like the person is in a snowstorm, I call this a "Snowy Mirror Picture." They might look super hot, but no one will be able to tell through all the fingerprints and spittle. Is it really that difficult to wipe a mirror off before snapping a picture? They might also need to clean up the room a bit. Nobody wants to see a pile of dirty underwear in the background. Nobody. And no one has ever put "slob" in the pro category.

I've taken a picture of myself to demonstrate:

14
YOU KNOW WHAT PISSES ME OFF??

When you leave someone a voice mail but they don't listen to it.

I could never do this because that little notification annoys the crap out of me. But to each his own. What really bugs me is when I leave someone an important voice mail with important details, and that person calls me back without even listening to it! Then I have to repeat myself and say it all over again! What was the point of leaving the voice mail in the first place?! Voice mail was created for a reason!

Voicemail

See this little notification? It means I left you a voice mail and you should listen to it to find out why I called.

15

YOU KNOW WHAT PISSES ME OFF??

The call-and-run.

This is when someone calls you, but you miss the call by a second. Then you call them back within two seconds, and they don't answer. WHY? Did me not answering their call cause them to go into a hysterical frenzy making them chuck their phone into the black abyss of the sea and run for the hills?

I'll call them, text them, leave voice mails, but they won't respond. I become obsessed with needing to know why they called. WHY WON'T THEY RESPOND?! Then I start freaking out and make up crazy scenarios of why they didn't answer:

1. Maybe they were dying and called me for help but then passed out!
2. What if a kidnapper took them and said that they had one call but no more, then I missed it and the kidnapper killed them?!
3. What if they were on *Who Wants to Be a Millionaire,* and I was their one phone call and could have won them a million dollars, but I missed it and now they'll be poor forever?!
4. What if they got stranded in the middle of the desert, and they used the last of their battery power to call me, then the phone died before I could call back?!
5. What if they were calling because they won an all-expenses-paid vacation around the world that was leaving right that instant, and they could bring one person with them but that person had to pick up the phone RIGHT THEN! And unbeknownst to them, I was finishing the last bite of my Costco pizza and wanted to finish chewing before talking on the phone. And now they're gone, and I've just missed out on the chance of a lifetime!

Clearly, I freak out about these things. Just pick up the phone when I call back.

16
YOU KNOW WHAT PISSES ME OFF??

When people tell me their dreams.

First off, I just hate dreams in general. It's either a nightmare, which is obviously terrible, or they are great and magical, which are awesome when you're asleep but SUCK once you wake up. Want to know why? Because they will NEVER come true. Your brain is basically teasing you, the little punk. But I absolutely HATE when I hear the 5 words "in my dream last night." Also, I want to slap people who get mad at someone because of something he or she did in a dream. Do you not realize it wasn't actually that person doing anything? Dreams are pointless, and therefore, I don't want to hear about them. Stop telling me about them. Go away!

17

YOU KNOW WHAT PISSES ME OFF??

When people don't understand when PMS happens.

I want to yell at anyone who says, "someone is on their period," to explain emotional behavior. Don't they know that PMS stands for "Pre-Menstrual Syndrome"? PRE-! Meaning BEFORE! A woman's hormones are out of whack before her period and go back to normal once it starts. I am no exception to this rule. I always want to cry one to two days before my period starts, but once it does, I'm back to being a sane human (well, as sane as I can get).

If you know a girl is on her period and simultaneously mad at you, she's not mad at you because she's on her period . . . she's mad at you because you're a dick.

If my words still didn't get it through your thick skull, I've included a calendar showing where PMS is in relation to a period.

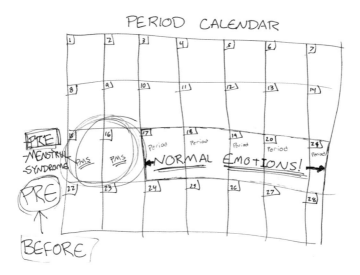

Oh! And one more thing. Telling a girl that she must be on her period, that she's PMS-ing, or that she is being overly emotional, has helped with nothing whatsoever in 100 percent of situations. Don't blame a woman's emotions on the lining of her uterus shedding, blame it on the fact that you suck as a human being.

18
YOU KNOW WHAT PISSES ME OFF??

When people say, "I don't care," but they really do.

If you ask someone what they want to eat, and they say, "I don't care," then they have forfeited their right to have an opinion on what you choose. Therefore, if you pick something and they reject your decision, THEY LIED!

They can be as picky as they want, as long as they never say, "I don't care." They should help make their own decision by telling you what they want, or eat whatever you order without complaining.

19

YOU KNOW WHAT PISSES ME OFF??

When people get mad at me for putting up my Christmas decorations "early."

Who made you the ruler of the universe? Why do you get to decide when I get to put up MY Christmas decorations? I'm not forcing you to put up your decorations. I'm not canceling Thanksgiving. If anything, I'm making my house look better for Thanksgiving. They take a lot of flippin' time and energy to put up and I want them to stay up as long as possible! Get over yourself—Merry Christmas, and a Happy New Year.

Here's this really amazing picture of my sister and me awkward-smiling while decorating my parents' Christmas tree together.

You're welcome.

20
YOU KNOW WHAT PISSES ME OFF??

When people let their pride get in the way of things.

Stop it. You're stupid. People should take pride in their amazing accomplishments that make the world a better place. For instance, heart surgeons can take pride in the fact that they've successfully taken the heart of a dead person and put it in the body of a dying person to make them not dying. A round of applause for them. But, if you're too proud to admit that you've done wrong, and you hurt people in return, then you're stupid.

I've seen so many people fight because someone won't let go of their pride, even though they are clearly in the wrong. This happens in so many areas of life: not backing down from a physical or verbal altercation, not accepting help, not accepting money, not admitting that you're wrong, etc. And sometimes being that prideful is really just you being stubborn and a brat.

For example, let's say there are four friends, three are comfortable in the amount of money they have, and one is lacking in the financial department. Nothing to be ashamed of, we've all been there. Let's call that one friend *Banana*. Now imagine all four friends are hanging out and one of the wealthier friends comes up with a fun activity for them all to do, but it costs a little more than the average adventure. The three financially stable friends all get SUPER excited, but Banana says the group can't do it because it's too expensive. The person who came up with the idea realizes it was a little rude to assume everyone could pay for it, so he/she insists on paying for the activity for everyone because it was their idea. Seems generous and sensible, correct? But then Banana still says no because they have too much pride to accept handouts from people. Therefore, none of the friends can go on the most epic adventure of their lives because Banana is too prideful.

See how that can be a total crotch shot to a good time? Gosh darn it, if someone is offering to pay for your Disneyland ticket, put on your dang Mickey ears and skip down Main Street! Obviously mooching isn't the best, and I can understand wanting to make it on your own, but sometimes you need to swallow your pride for the bigger picture.

YOU KNOW WHAT PISSES ME OFF??

When kids wiggle their teeth.

Don't get me wrong, I love a good wiggle: a wiggle of the booty, a whole body wiggle, or a slow finger wiggle (also known as a finger wag). But I do NOT support a tooth wiggle. It grosses me out!

Example: This is a picture of my nephew, Jacob. Cutest, nicest, and most epic kid on the planet. But whenever he gets a loose tooth and wants to show me, I RUN for the hills. I can't even handle this picture because I know his tooth is wiggly enough to fall out.

22
YOU KNOW WHAT PISSES ME OFF??

When people judge me for driving instead of walking.

I've had numerous cab drivers say to me, "you know, you could just walk there from here." Excuse me? Do your dang job and drive me! I know where I could walk! I have GPS on my phone! Maybe I'm in a hurry, maybe my foot hurts, maybe I have asthma, maybe I'm from Southern California where we drive everywhere because we have cars, wide roads, and convenient parking. YOU DON'T KNOW MY LIFE!

Cars move faster than humans, that's just science. I'm a person that likes to go fast and get things done quickly. Therefore, 9 times out of 10, I'm going to choose taking a vehicle over using my legs. I know a half mile will only take me 10 minutes to walk, but it will take a car less than 1 minute. That's 9 minutes saved! Nine minutes can make or break a lot of things! What if you were 9 minutes late to your plane—it's already taken off and you're stuck at the airport. What if you were 9 minutes late to the hospital and missed the birth of you first child? What if you were 9 minutes late to school? You all know you'd get written up for that for sure!

23
YOU KNOW WHAT PISSES ME OFF??

When people watch what I'm doing on my computer.

If you're my friend or family member, and I'm sitting next to you, I don't care if you look at what I'm doing; I have nothing to hide (for the most part). If you're a stranger sitting next to me on an airplane, that's a whole other story. Don't look at my computer. It's not your computer. What I'm doing is none of your concern. Look away! If we are on an airplane, you look at your screen on the seat back in front of you, or you look at your own entertainment that you brought for yourself. If you forgot entertainment, too bad!

24
YOU KNOW WHAT
PISSES ME OFF??

When people use the argument, "Not Adam and Steve."

When it was announced that gays were allowed to marry each other in all 50 states, people who did not agree with this law started throwing around the argument, "It's Adam and Eve! Not Adam and Steve!" They really used rhyme as their compelling argument. Smart.

But then again, there actually isn't a good argument against gay marriage, so I suppose rhyming was the only way to go.

25

YOU KNOW WHAT PISSES ME OFF??

When people think that Pepsi is the same as Coca-Cola.

I didn't ask for Pepsi; I asked for Coca-Cola. They are not the same thing. They don't taste the same. It's okay that you don't have Coke, just don't assume that Pepsi is a substitute. That's like an English teacher asking me for an essay and me being like, "Oh yeah, I actually don't have an essay, but I do have some math homework, that should work, right?" IT'S NOT THE SAME!

Coca-Cola
≠
Pepsi

26
YOU KNOW WHAT PISSES ME OFF??

When pregnant women use weeks instead of months.

If I ask you how far along you are, and you say, "17 weeks," I have no clue how long that is. I'm obviously aware that it's 17 weeks, but I don't know how many months that is. Sure, I could do a little math, which would only take me a few moments. Or, you could just say, "a little over 4 months." Then I would know you're about halfway through your pregnancy and zero math is required on my part. I'm not the pregnant one, why should I do any work? I'd love to help out pregnant women in any other way, but don't make me do your baby math.

When people point out my typos.

Do you think this makes you smart or funny? Half the time it's AutoCorrect that's an idiot and changes a word on me, so why are you correcting me? Unless you're correcting a school essay, why must you correct a typo? The only thing correcting my grammar or typos does is make me hate you.

Whenever I make a typo in a tweet, the only responses I get are from people correcting that typo. My initial reaction is to block those people for being evil spawns of Satan, but I've learned that I should go to their pages and see what kind of people they are first. And what I've discovered is that most of these punks can't tweet a single tweet without there being 12 typos involved. And they point out my ONE typo every HUNDRED tweets?! Nah bro. Don't play me like that. My hatred for hypocrites is a topic for another book.

When people give me advice that I didn't ask for.

If I ask for your advice, then by all means, talk my ear off. But if you randomly just walk up to me and tell me how to live my life—no.

If you come up to me, while I'm eating my extra-greasy, non-farm-fresh, unnatural, double-meat pizza, to tell me that I'm harming my good "gut bacteria," I'm going to shove a loaf of gluten-free bread down your throat. Keep your knowledge to yourself.

Now I want pizza. Dang it.

29
YOU KNOW WHAT PISSES ME OFF??

When people drive slow in the fast lane.

When driving on the freeway, it's important to know that the right lane is the slow lane and the left lane is the fast lane, or "the passing lane." Despite the speed limits, that's just the rule. Even cops know this! There are signs on freeways and highways that say SLOW TRAFFIC KEEP RIGHT. The government knows! Therefore, if you're cruising in the far left lane going 65 in a 65 mph zone when there is no one in front of you, I HATE YOU! By all means, drive the speed limit! BUT IN THE APPROPRIATE LANE!

You actually cause traffic to back up by going that slow in the fast lane. I also wholeheartedly believe that doing that causes accidents. Think about the people who go 80 mph on the freeway: those are probably the same people who aren't afraid to weave in and out of traffic. Therefore, if you're going super slow in the super-fast lane, fast people are going to try and pass you. The more people change lanes, the more accidents happen. Boom! Science.

Below is how I think freeway speeds should be:

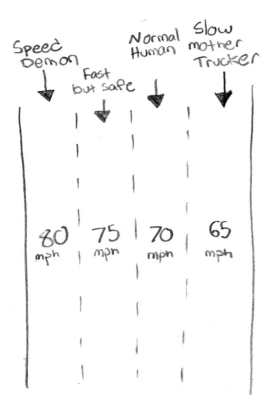

TYPES OF PEOPLE

30

YOU KNOW WHAT PISSES ME OFF??

Morning people.

People that can just wake up and be super peppy are the worst kinds of people. They can't be trusted.

Don't talk to me in the morning. Don't even look at me. Why would you think this is an appropriate time to ask me how I am? Clearly, I'm not well, I just had to wake up and leave the comfort and warmth of my bed. Also, what could you possibly have to talk about!? We've just woken up! Nothing has happened!! And if you're about to say you want to talk about the dream that you just had . . . well, I think I've already made my feelings on that clear enough.

Except for my best friend, who made me put this part in: She is a great person and I love her even though she is a morning person who often texts me at 6 a.m.

31
YOU KNOW WHAT PISSES ME OFF??

Sexist people.

Notice that I didn't say sexist "men," and that's because women can be sexist, too. I think it's time that people get out of the mind-set that people should or shouldn't do something based on what type of genitalia they have. If I want to build a house, me and my vagina are going to build a dang house! If a boy wants to wear makeup, I say, "PLEASE DO!" I don't want to be staring at those zits! Not that I find them gross, I actually don't mind them at all, but they are just hard to look away from!

I get great pleasure out of proving sexist people wrong. One time a man told me that men naturally have a better sense of direction. I scoffed. He then tried to prove me wrong by asking which way was north. I pointed one way, he pointed another. We got out a compass and I took a celebratory drink of a cold beer. Win.

As a kid I was into a wide variety of activities that were often characterized as "boy" things. But that didn't stop me. Every day, I put on my cargo pants and filled them with bouncy balls, fake knives, money, and a first aid kit. Then I went out to play in my tree house with my Rottweiler and G.I. Joes.

Smelly people.

Now listen, I know that every once in a while every person will emit a little stink. Even me. Sometimes your deodorant wears off, your workout was extra hard, or something spilled on you. However, when you are CONSISTENTLY smelly 24/7, then we have a problem. In this world we have deodorant, perfume, cologne, lotion, gum, breath mints, toothpaste, mouthwash, showers, soap, shampoo, conditioner, laundry detergent, washers and dryers, fabric softener, and the list just goes on and on. There are few to NO excuses for being consistently stinky! I don't care if the stank from your body doesn't bother you, it bothers ME!!! And let's face it, I care more about my comfort than yours. Why would you smell bad when you could smell good? My brain just doesn't comprehend that.

And you wonder why there are always flies buzzing around you. You smell like poop, that's why. POOP!

I've taken a picture of all the things I use to make sure I don't smell bad, just in case there is a person out there who doesn't believe that these things exist, or is confused about what they look like.

33

YOU KNOW WHAT PISSES ME OFF??

Joke stealers.

I've cracked one or two jokes in my day. I've even gotten a laugh from one of them. And I don't care if people use my jokes—spread the laughter, by all means. But, my friend, give credit where credit is due. This may sound childish, and that's because it is. I just want people to know I'm funny, dang it! If I tell you a joke, then you literally turn around and tell it to the person behind you and they laugh and say you're the funniest person ever . . . you're letting that person live in a world of lies. You're not the funniest person ever, I am. And, of course, I can't jump in and say, "That was actually my joke," because then I just look like sour grapes. But as I've gotten older, I've realized that I don't care if I look like sour grapes, as long as I also look funny.

34
YOU KNOW WHAT PISSES ME OFF??

Drunk drivers.

Are people really still doing this? If you drunk-drive, I actually have zero respect for you as a human being. There are cabs, buses, the subway; there's Uber, Lyft, and anyone in your contact list on your phone that you could call for a ride home. With how often people die from drunk drivers, you'd think it would stop. But no, people are really just that stupid and inconsiderate. Imagine someone you love, walking down the street or driving in a car, doing absolutely nothing wrong, then being murdered because some idiot had one too many drinks and didn't want to leave their car and pick it up in the morning. Screw that person. Don't drink and drive. If you do, I hate you.

35
YOU KNOW WHAT PISSES ME OFF??

People who are always late.

If you tell me you'll be somewhere at a certain time, I expect you to be there at that time. Obviously, a few minutes late is okay; I live in a place where parking can be hard to find. But being more than 15 minutes late is irritating. Do I look like I got time to spare? Do I look like I enjoy waiting for you?

If you take only one thing away from the billion years you spent in school, let it be that you have to be on time. The end.

36

YOU KNOW WHAT PISSES ME OFF??

Line cutters.

Why do you think you're more special than me? My mama actually told me that I'm the most special, so if you think you are, then you are sadly mistaken. You have no right to cut in line. People have been waiting, we all have the same goal, we are all humans, and society says we have to wait in line. And whether you like it or not, you are part of this society; therefore, you have to wait in line like the rest of us! Also, even if you ask one person if you can cut in front of them and they say it's okay, it's still not okay, because you have not asked the 50 other people behind them that it is also affecting. You think you are so polite because you got permission from one person, but what about the rest of us!? Most line cutters know that the majority of people will not confront them—it's awkward and you'll look petty—but unfortunately for any line cutter out there, I am not most people. I will yell, I will bring attention to you and your rule-breaking self, and I will make you get to your rightful place . . . THE BACK OF THE LINE!

YOU KNOW WHAT PISSES ME OFF??

Slow people.

I'm not talking about people with disabilities (I'm not a dick). I'm talking about people who just move slow for no reason.

I move at a pace which I think is reasonable and also happens to be fast. Why would you ever move slowly? Don't you have things to do? The faster you move, the faster things get done. If things get done fast, then you have time for other things. People always say, "Slow down and enjoy life. Smell the roses. You might miss something if you're speeding through life." I disagree with that. Move quick, get your stuff done, then you'll be able to smell the roses without the pressure of your to-do list hanging over your head.

One other point: if you move slow, you'll be late for stuff, which will annoy me even more!

CERTAIN SOCIAL NORMS

38 YOU KNOW WHAT PISSES ME OFF??

How society has declared that all farts are gross.

I understand that if a fart smells, the smell is always a bad smell. None of us have ever smelled a good-smelling fart. But if I fart and it doesn't smell, why is that gross? And if you're going to argue about "poop particles," do you think I'm running around naked, in public, farting? Clearly those poop particles would end up in my undies and not in your mouth. Just let me fart my odorless farts in peace. If you don't, then my stomach will start hurting, and I'll have to wiggle around making really weird faces while I try to figure out a position that will allow my fart to come out silently.

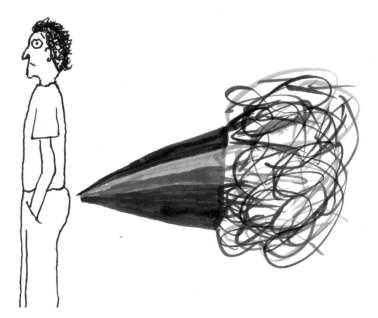

See, farts can be beautiful.

39

YOU KNOW WHAT PISSES ME OFF??

That society has declared sticking your tongue out as the universal "silly face."

Look through any group photo you've ever taken where the group decided to take a "silly picture"—there will be at least one person in that picture sticking out their tongue. I do it from time to time because that is what society has taught me to do. But I need to know why! It's not silly! It's unsanitary, if anything! Just putting your tongue out there in the world! Letting air particles stick to it!

Next time you take a "silly picture," resist the urge and try something new.

40
YOU KNOW WHAT PISSES ME OFF??

That society doesn't accept cereal as a proper dinner.

It's FINE for breakfast and tolerated for lunch, but the second that clock strikes 5:00 p.m., NOPE! Unacceptable!

It doesn't make sense! It's food!! Shouldn't we be able to eat it anytime? Who decided what breakfast food is and why we can only eat it in the morning? I love cereal. It's delicious. And a massive bowl of cereal drenched in cold milk fills me up and makes my taste buds happy. Does it lose its nutritional value as the day gets later but gain it back once the clock strikes midnight? What is this Cinderella cereal lie?

41
YOU KNOW WHAT PISSES ME OFF??

That people really think we need to learn cursive.

Other than to sign important legal documents, what's the point?

There is always that one turd-face who thinks they are super-sophisticated because they only write in cursive. I want to fart on that person's eyeball. Reading their notes is like reading a foreign language. I know what the words say, it just takes me extra seconds to translate them to what I understand. Why would you do that to me? I'm trying to cheat off you here; don't make me use my brain! That's what I'm trying to avoid!

Here's a z just to zest things up, because no one knows what a z is in cursive.

That society has decided that eyebrows need to be "on fleek."

Who decided that eyebrows can't just be normal hair on a face? Now eyebrows gotta be plucked, shaped, shaded, threaded, drawn, and "on fleek."

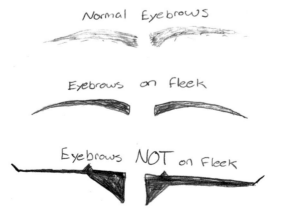

I've been told I have good eyebrows, but I have no idea what that even means. That compliment is lost on me. I always knew that a unibrow was bad, but I didn't know there were other things that could go wrong with those tiny patches of hair. They are so small and random but make SUCH an impact on the face!

43
YOU KNOW WHAT PISSES ME OFF??

That society says I can't pick a wedgie in public.

Because, guess what? I'm gonna pick it anyway. Why should I walk around with my underwear shoved up my butt crack? That's uncomfortable. I'm gonna pick that bundle right out of there no matter where I am. And it's gonna feel so good.

Seriously, though, society tells me to wear a thong, then gets pissed when I try to make it a little less uncomfortable. No thank you. I'll wear your thong, sir, but I will also pick it from my buttocks!

Tipping.

In America, you are supposed to tip. That's what we've decided. Therefore, I tip. Always. Regardless of service. That, right there, is a fact that I hate. Why would I be an asshole for not tipping when the service was absolutely terrible?

I understand that servers in the USA get paid based on the fact that they will get tips. But, if you did your job terribly, why do I have to give you more money that is supposed to be a reward for great service? This hasn't stopped me from tipping, though. I always tip 20 percent because I don't want to be a douche bag, but I'm not happy about it! And who decides this percentage? I need to know which group of humans got together and decided that between 15 percent and 20 percent of the total on the check is how much I should tip. I feel like I should have gotten a say in this madness.

And before you get mad at me for my thoughts on this—I've worked in a restaurant and lived off of tips. That doesn't mean I understand them.

45
YOU KNOW WHAT PISSES ME OFF??

That nose picking isn't acceptable.

When someone has a booger hanging out of their nose, it's all anyone is going to notice. They will be stared at. It's embarrassing for them and everyone in the room. But that person probably wouldn't have that booger situation if it was okay to pick our noses in public. I agree boogers are gross, but I still want to be able to pick my nose whenever I want! It's satisfying! And don't act like you don't enjoy it as well.

And let's just put this out in the public space: picking your nose with a bare finger feels 1000 percent better than picking with a tissue. Science.

46

Waiting for everyone to get
their food before I can start eating.

I hate that rule. I don't want to eat cold food because your food is late! I want to eat my food when it is at the perfect temperature. Why must I suffer because the waiter hates you? I'm hungry! I've never been angry at someone for eating before my food arrives. Why would I? If anything, I just steal a bite of theirs, and then, once I get my food, they can have a bite of mine! There, problem solved. That way we can all eat warm food!

That peeing in the shower in frowned upon.

Come on, it all goes to the same place. It's sterile. It gets washed away! Everybody needs to calm down about it. It feels so good to do, too. It's the only time I get to pee standing up! Men get to pee standing up all the time; let me have this one thing.

And don't you dare say you've never peed in the shower! Everybody does it, just no one wants to admit it. If you're that one strange person out there who has never done it, you don't know what you're missing.

OBJECTS / THINGS

48
YOU KNOW WHAT
PISSES ME OFF??

"Wireless" chargers.

THEY AREN'T WIRELESS! You still have to plug the charging station into something! Also, they make it so you can't use your phone while it's charging! You can't trick me into thinking this new device is groundbreaking.

The commercials for them try to fool you with trickery, showing you videos of people trying to plug in their chargers at the airport and failing. But they never show the people using wireless chargers at the airport because it would be the exact same situation! You have to plug in the charging station!

49
YOU KNOW WHAT PISSES ME OFF??

Kids' Band-Aids.

You'd think that kids' Band-Aids would stick better because kids are more active. But NO!!! One ounce of sweat and you'll find that brightly colored cartoon sticker flapping about, hanging on by a hair. A literal hair on your leg. Then you realize you have poor grooming habits and should probably shave once in a while.

Assistive Touch on iPhones.

iPhones have this little white circle thing that sits on the screen,

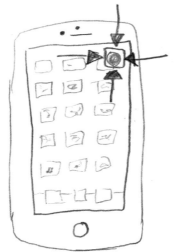

and when you touch it, different options pop up on the screen:

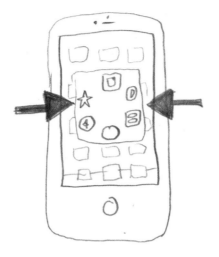

But the thing is, NO ONE USES THIS OR INVITED IT TO BE ON THE SCREEN! I have turned this thing off maybe 784 times, and somehow it ALWAYS finds its way back onto my screen! And when I'm trying to take a selfie, its witchcraft always manages to put itself right over the button you press to take the photo. So when I try to capture my beauty, I get an option to go to another app. SCREW YOURSELF, ASSISTIVE TOUCH!

Pockets on girl jeans.

I think the purse companies got together with the pants companies and decided to make girls' pockets really small so we have to buy purses. Ladies, have you stuck your hand in a man's pocket lately? THEY HAVE SO MUCH MORE ROOM THAN OURS! I'm not saying I would use all that space, but I'd like the option. Whenever I try to stick something in the pocket of my jeans, the object just pops right out while I'm walking or drops in the toilet when I pull down my pants to pee! Unacceptable!

Here is a diagram of boys' pants pockets versus girls' pants pockets:

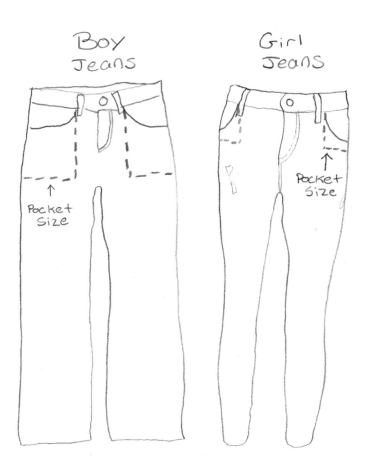

Side note: I'm also angry that girls' jackets don't have pockets on the inside. Guys get all the pocket fun.

52

YOU KNOW WHAT PISSES ME OFF??

Coleslaw.

I'll just never understand it. Why would I eat that?

YOU KNOW WHAT PISSES ME OFF??

Cars without cup holders.

Cars should ALWAYS have one cup holder per seat, then one extra in case I get super thirsty and want two drinks. Or, in the event I'm being super nice and have bought someone else a drink.

They used to not put cup holders in cars at all, and people were forced to get real creative. I've seat-belted drinks in, stuck them in the crack between the seat and divider, and even gotten these contraptions that hang from the window for drinks to sit in. Then cup holders were all the rage and everyone loved them! No more spilled drinks and DIY makeshift holders! But somehow they are slowly dying out again. Stop that! My car should be able to drive me from point A to point B while holding all my liquids!

Hotel hallway carpet.

Why are hotel hallways lined with THICK carpeting? Why would you install the toughest flooring to roll a suitcase over in an area where you are expecting to have high suitcase traffic?

Have you ever gotten off a thirteen-hour flight from America to New Zealand, super exhausted and so excited to get to your hotel room and go to sleep, only to step off the elevator to realize that the little amount of energy you have left that was going to go towards taking your pants off and brushing your teeth will actually be used to help get your two massive suitcases from the elevator to your room? If it was tile or even thin carpet, it would take no effort at all. But that thick plushy carpet is there to mock you and laugh at you, making fun of your arms for not being able to roll a bag designed for rolling.

Warning: If this ever happens to you, resist the urge to kick the bags. You'll end up looking even more foolish and have a limp for a couple days.

55

YOU KNOW WHAT PISSES ME OFF??

AutoCorrect.

Don't get me wrong, AutoCorrect has helped me out of a lot of jams, but it has also made me look like a complete idiot in a number of situations.

If I'm telling someone to f*** off, I'm definitely not telling them to "duck off." AutoCorrect has this annoying habit of changing correctly spelled words into something completely different. Stop that. And when I erase it to try to write the word again, it keeps changing it. I'm yelling at my phone for a good thirty seconds while I figure out how to convince it to stay on the right word.

56
YOU KNOW WHAT PISSES ME OFF??

Honeydew and cantaloupe.

No one likes you. You serve no purpose but to take up room in my fruit salad so they don't have to pay for more good-tasting fruit. Go away bad fruit. The only people who actually like those fruits are probably also morning people. So untrustworthy.

Soup.

This is going to sound weird to a lot of you, but I don't think soup is a meal; it's a hot liquid with chunks in it, which is really unappetizing.

You can either dunk bread into soup, so it acts as a dip, or you can drink it. You can't eat it. There are chunks of food in it that you can eat, but the soup itself, you drink. Also, no one has ever been full after a bowl of soup. It's not a meal, so don't try to pass it off as one.

Sleep.

Just the fact that we need it. I love being asleep, but I hate that I have to sleep. It's not a luxury, it's a requirement. So inconvenient! And no matter how much sleep I get, I always seem to be tired! Why can't my body learn to recharge itself while I'm awake and watching TV. I think that's a much better plan. I really should have been consulted when the human being was being developed.

59

YOU KNOW WHAT PISSES ME OFF??

Treadmill commercials.

Why are the people in those commercials always using a treadmill on the top of a mountain? How did they get it up there? How is it plugged in? That must be one long extension cord.

No one looks that happy on a treadmill, either. Those smiles aren't fooling anybody. If you're on a treadmill, you're going to be sweaty and look like you're about to die. That's just how it is.

Wax napkins.

I hate the napkins that are basically wax paper. They don't clean up anything. They seem to just smear it around a bit. And you think getting more napkins will help, but you just end up smearing stuff around even more. It would be more useful to use your bare hands.

Romantic movies.

Romantic movies present a false representation of real relationships, and they have the most predictable plots in the entire world.

These movies make girls think that guys are supposed to do over-the-top romantic gestures, but in reality, if a guy actually ever did any of those things, you would find it awkward and creepy.

Have you ever had a guy on a guitar try to sing you a love song? It's so awkward. Where are you supposed to look? You can't make eye contact. But you seem rude if you're not looking at him. It's mortifying and not sexy.

Romantic Movies —

Reality —

Pointless pets.

Why do people own fish? What's the point? You can't pet them, and they don't have personalities. Well, they might have personalities, but they just reset every 3 seconds.

Whenever I sec a fish tank, I begin to question the meaning of life. Real hippie stuff starts coming out of my mouth: "Are we all just fish in a tank? Swimming around in circles with no purpose?" I can't help it, though! It looks so depressing! I look at a dog and all I see is happiness! A caged bird or a fish: just sadness.

63

Naps.

Since I was a kid, I've always hated naps. Things happen in the middle of the day, so if I doze off while the sun is up, I might miss something exciting.

Naps also mess with my sleep schedule. If I take a nap during the day, there's no way on earth that I'm falling asleep at a decent hour that night.

AND ANOTHER THING! When I wake up from a nap, I have absolutely no idea what's going on. Especially if I fall asleep when the sun is out and wake up after the sun has set. I feel like someone who's just woken from being in a coma for 6 months and doesn't know what year it is. I've forgotten my own name after a nap! They don't do the mind good.

64
YOU KNOW WHAT PISSES ME OFF??

Radio commercials.

Have you ever heard a funny radio commercial in your entire life? I can answer that for you—no, you haven't. Radio commercials have to be the most annoying form of advertising out there, and yet stations continue to use them.

Also, what is with those scripts?! They're more unnatural than cheese from a can! And there's that ridiculously sped up fast-talking guy at the end who tells you all the things wrong with the product and what it might do to you, like give you oily flatulence!

65

YOU KNOW WHAT PISSES ME OFF??

Scary movie commercials.

I did NOT consent to see them!!! I hate scary movies more than anything else on this planet (there is a slight chance I may be overexaggerating a little bit), so therefore, I do not watch them. But sometimes, when I'm watching a family-friendly show all happy and content, it goes to commercial, THEN OUT OF NOWHERE A DOLL MAN-CHILD COMES OUT OF THE STOMACH OF A VAMPIRE DEAD OLD LADY WITH A CHAINSAW TRYING TO SUCK THE SOULS OUT OF COLLEGE STUDENTS IN THE MIDDLE OF THE WOODS OUTSIDE A HAUNTED MANSION! I DIDN'T CONSENT TO SEE THAT! How is that legal!? I repeat, I did not consent to that!

66

YOU KNOW WHAT PISSES ME OFF??

Childhood cancer.

All cancer sucks, but cancer in kids makes me the saddest and angriest. Children shouldn't have to worry about dying. They should be playing outside and complaining about having to go to school.

I've met so many great, amazing kids who had to grow up way too fast because their childhoods ended the second they got diagnosed with cancer. They had to chin up and deal with the idea of their lives ending before they even got their first kiss. Had to witness the people around them grieve their death while they're still alive. It's not right.

Go donate. The end.

67
YOU KNOW WHAT PISSES ME OFF??

Gross words.

We all know the list of gross words:

1. Moist
2. Crevice
3. Penetrate
4. Slurp
5. Soggy
6. Crusty
7. Erect
8. Gyrate
9. Puss
10. Panties
11. Gesticulate

12. Ointment
13. Squirt
14. Slit
15. Fungi
16. Crease

Say them slowly, out loud. You'll see what I mean.
People need to stop saying these words.

Recommended serving sizes.

Why are the recommended serving sizes so ridiculously small? We all know that we aren't stopping at 3 cookies or at 10 chips.

When I glance at the nutritional facts, they seem not half bad, then I realize that the recommended serving size for that frosting is 1 teaspoon. COME ON! In what world does someone use one teaspoon of frosting?

Nutrition Facts

Serving Size 1 tsp (6g)

Servings Per Container about 30

Amount Per Serving

Calories 25   Calories from Fat 10

	% Daily Value*
Total Fat 1g	2%
Sodium 5mg	0%
Total Carb. 4g	1%
Sugars 3g	
Protein 0g	

Not a significant source of saturated fat, trans fat, cholesterol, dietary fiber, vitamin A, vitamin C, calcium and iron.

*Percent Daily Values are based on a 2,000 calorie diet.

Nutrition Facts

Serving Size 1 tsp (6g)

Servings Per Container about 30

YOU KNOW WHAT PISSES ME OFF??

Retail stickers.

Why on earth do retailers put these massive, indestructible stickers on merchandise that they are trying to sell at half price?! Oh great, that kitchen thingy is marked down! BUT AT WHAT PRICE?! The price of you having to sit and scratch off the markdown sticker for 30 minutes! That sticker might be scratching off but so is the skin on your fingers!

SCREW YOU, STICKER!

EVERYTHING ELSE

70

YOU KNOW WHAT PISSES ME OFF??

That hitting a fly doesn't kill it . . .

. . . it just kind of pushes it around a little bit. Then you have to deal with the fact that you touched a fly that is born in feces and it's flying around bugging the living sh*t out of you.

High Five, Bro! Buzzzz

71
YOU KNOW WHAT PISSES ME OFF??

The fact that dragons never existed.

How is that possible!? It totally seems plausible.

Fun fact: until I was 23, I thought dragons had actually existed. . . .

72

YOU KNOW WHAT
PISSES ME OFF??

The fact that "Bob" is short for "Robert."

Who decided that?! It doesn't make sense! Rob is short for Robert. Bob is short for Bobby. Done. Logic.

73

YOU KNOW WHAT PISSES ME OFF??

Eating grapes with a fork.

IT IS SO HARD! They slip away from the fork and fling across the room! (Don't ask me why I tried eating grapes with a fork. They are clearly a finger food.)

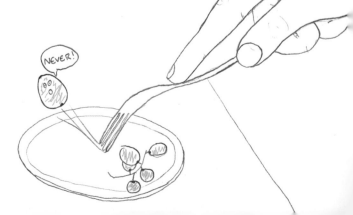

74

YOU KNOW WHAT PISSES ME OFF??

When I eat all my food.

Because then it's gone and I have to wait until the next meal to eat again. Even if I'm full, I'm still sad that it's gone forever. I loved that food, and I thought it loved me, too. But then it disappeared and left me sitting alone in sadness.

I think that's why I love leftovers so much. The next day I'm reminded that my food does love me, and there is more for me to love back. Until I eat all the leftovers—then I'm sad again.

75
YOU KNOW WHAT
PISSES ME OFF??

The never ending AC battle in my car.

I'm too cold with the AC on, but too hot with it off. I can never seem to find that middle sweet spot. Does it even exist? Is it even possible? Am I doomed forever?

Poop splash.

You know what I'm talking about: when you drop a short but heavy one in the toilet and it hits the water so hard that the water splashes back up onto your butt cheeks. It's gross. It's hard not to imagine the remnants of past poops made by other people still floating around in the water, which is now dripping from your buns.

YOU KNOW WHAT PISSES ME OFF??

Getting ready for bed.

The worst is when you've somehow crawled into bed without getting ready for bed and start to fall asleep. You might have been on the phone, started watching TV and then got cold, or you were doing your homework in bed. Doesn't matter how it happened, but you got under those covers without brushing your teeth or putting your PJs on. Then, when it's time to deal with yourself, you have to get out of bed to get ready for bed. You're so tired, but then you uncover yourself, letting in a gust of cold air that perks you right awake.

78

YOU KNOW WHAT PISSES ME OFF??

The phrase "if you love something, let it go."

No! If I love something, I'm keeping it forever! I love my mom, which means she's never allowed to die. Ever. That's the rule. My boyfriend is never allowed to break up with me. No one in my family is allowed to move out of California, and I always have to live near an In-N-Out Burger. I love these things, so they have to stay close to me. If I don't love something, then I let it go.

YOU KNOW WHAT PISSES ME OFF??

The noise of opening a soda can.

How is it the loudest noise on planet earth? There is no discreet way to do it. Open a soda can in a room full of people—no matter how loud that room is, everyone will hear it.

HEY! EVERYBODY! LOOK! I'M BEING OPENED! YAY! NOISE!

YOU KNOW WHAT PISSES ME OFF??

The lack of shelving in public bathrooms.

Most of the time, women will have a purse or bag on them. So when public restrooms for women don't have a place to put that bag, I get angry. But that's not the only reason I'm angry. Oh no. If I'm on the toilet, I'm going to be looking at my phone, and when it comes time to wipe, I'm going to want to put my phone down. So if I don't have a secure place to put my phone, like the top of a boxy toilet paper dispenser, I'm going to freak out!

81

YOU KNOW WHAT PISSES ME OFF??

The fact that I still need quarters to do my laundry.

Quarters are like gold to me. I don't care about how much money I have in the government-insured bank, I care about how many quarters I have in my piggy bank.

I will never be that person who says, "Keep the change." That change is mine.

82
YOU KNOW WHAT
PISSES ME OFF??

The fact that *Friends* ended.

That was a dang good show! I could watch any episode at any time and laugh. WHY DID IT HAVE TO END?

83

YOU KNOW WHAT PISSES ME OFF??

Reality show recaps.

Why do reality shows need to recap that last two minutes of what just happened before the commercial break? Do they really think we forgot EVERYTHING that happened during the 30 seconds it took them to advertise car insurance? Do they really have that little faith in us?

84
YOU KNOW WHAT PISSES ME OFF??

How microwave ovens make SO much noise.

WHY?! WHY DO THEY MAKE THE LOUDEST BEEPING NOISES IN THE WORLD EVERY TIME YOU PRESS A BUTTON!

I understand that once it's done cooking, the timer goes off; that's what happens in a kitchen. But why does every single button have to make noise? Let's be real—most of the time when we're using a microwave, everyone in the house is asleep and we're heating up some guilty pleasure food. You don't need everyone in the house waking up and hearing that! That's your business! Not theirs! There should be a silent option. Can someone get a smart person on that, please?

85
YOU KNOW WHAT PISSES ME OFF??

How hard knees are to shave.

I swear I'll spend 10 minutes trying to shave every centimeter of my knee. Then the second I dry off, I'll see an inch-long hair just chillin' there! How does it do that?!

Also, I got way too into drawing that chair.

86
YOU KNOW WHAT PISSES ME OFF??

The fact that I can't edit my tweets.

If Facebook has the ability, Twitter should have it, too. It doesn't make sense! Why does a social media site all about words not let you edit them? I'm tired of tweeting things that have a typo, then having to take the tweets down and retweet them with the typo fixed. It's not fun—not because of the work involved, but because my entire Twitter notification feed becomes filled with kids saying, "I saw that!" "I screen shotted that typo!" "You had a typo in the first one you posted!" "Why'd you repost this?" "SAW THAT!" "I saw you do that Rachel."

I choose not to look at Twitter those days.

87

YOU KNOW WHAT PISSES ME OFF??

Never-ending cleaning.

Cleaning is never done. You will always have to clean. There will always be *something* to clean. It never stops. NEVER! You just made your bed . . . you're gonna have to do that again tomorrow morning. And the next day. And the day after that one, too. Just finished your laundry? What about the clothes you were wearing while you did laundry? Those are dirty now.

IT NEVER ENDS!

88

YOU KNOW WHAT PISSES ME OFF??

The fact Subway messes up my sandwich.

With the way Subway is set up, it seems impossible for them to mess up. Except, it happens all the time. They've even given me the wrong sandwich altogether! HOW DOES THAT HAPPEN? I went through the entire line ordering my sandwich to perfection, then they wrapped it up and handed it to me. When I opened it up, it was a completely different sandwich. SORCERY!

But really, you tell them step-by-step how to make your sandwich, but sometimes they don't pay attention and put the wrong stuff on, then get pissed at you when you correct them.

89
YOU KNOW WHAT PISSES ME OFF??

When typos ruin a joke.

You could tweet the funniest joke of all time. A joke to put all other jokes to shame. But if you misspell one single word, it's over. It's done. You can't redeem yourself. It's no longer funny. Because people are dicks, they are no longer thinking about the joke, they are just thinking about the typo. And so are you.

Let's take a moment of silence for all those jokes out there that were killed by a typo.

silence

Thank you.

90
YOU KNOW WHAT PISSES ME OFF??

How convincing I am in the morning.

In the morning, I am the most convincing person on the planet. I've talked myself into sleeping through work, school, Disneyland, catching a flight, appointments with doctors, and much more.

I could be the best lawyer ever as long as I was arguing a case to get someone more sleep . . . unless the trial was in the morning, in which case I would definitely sleep through it.

91
YOU KNOW WHAT PISSES ME OFF??

How much work it is to be healthy.

To be healthy, you have to eat healthy and be active. Easy, right? Wrong. Because all of that is annoying, and I'd rather not do any of those things.

Eating healthy usually means you have to make meals yourself, and it's not going to be easy. You also have to decide what kind of healthy you are going to be. A muscle nut that only wants protein? A vegan? A vegetarian? Someone who only eats all-natural, cage-free, farm-fresh foods? Someone who cuts out carbs? Gluten free? Liquid diet? No white food? No sugars? Only green foods?

Also, if you're going to go down this ill-advised path, you'd better figure out what kind of healthy you want to be, because once you tell people, "No thanks on the cake, I'm trying to eat healthy," you're going to have 400 people telling you how you're doing it wrong.

Waiting for food to cool before eating it.

I hate that I'm so impatient that I can't wait for food to cool down before eating it. Somehow I think that I can handle the heat. Then the next day, the roof of my mouth is peeling off. Why do I take a bite of hot food and try to cool it off while it sits in my mouth burning me? We all do it. You open your mouth and breath out as if you were trying to fog a mirror. You look like a complete idiot. You could have just blown on the food before you put it in your mouth. It would have saved you the pain and the embarrassment. But you just couldn't wait. I burn my mouth about once a week on a baked potato. And yes, I eat baked potatoes about once a week.

93
YOU KNOW WHAT
PISSES ME OFF??

How my fingertips feel after I cut my fingernails.

I'm not talking about how my fingernails feel, I'm talking about the tips of my fingers—the part that hasn't touched anything in a while because my fingernails were so long that they blocked everything from touching the skin.

94
YOU KNOW WHAT PISSES ME OFF??

When your arm forgets you got a haircut.

If you've ever had long hair, then got a couple inches cut off, you've had this happen. The muscle memory in your arm doesn't register that your hair is gone, so when you hit the end of your hair with your brush, your arm goes swinging down and you look silly! Your arm eventually gets used to the cut, but for the first couple days, you look like someone who has never combed hair before.

95
YOU KNOW WHAT PISSES ME OFF??

Overpacking.

I'm the queen of it. I'll be going on a one-night trip back to my parents' house, but for some reason I'll think I need to pack a snowsuit, bikini, prom dress, TV, coffeemaker, and 3 pairs of pants.

I won't use 90 percent of what I packed, but somehow, I always manage to forget something important. Like underwear. I'm a genius.

That women are constantly leaking.

There is always something leaking out of our vaginas. And no one talks about it. It's taboo! But the world needs to know that our vaginas have a constant runny nose. We don't enjoy it! We can't stop it! It isn't pleasant! We don't like pulling down our pants to pee and seeing this clear/white crap in our undies, then pulling our pants back up and it's wet and cold 'cause our underwear was down too long and is no longer body temperature!

Sometimes when I don't want to deal with it, I shove a tampon up there so my undies stay nice and dry. Which apparently is bad for you and can cause toxic shock syndrome. But that's how much I hate it—I'm willing to risk my life so I don't have to deal with discharge for a night.

Suck it world. I talked about it.

97

YOU KNOW WHAT PISSES ME OFF??

When I want something but it's over there.

That's just too far away.

98

YOU KNOW WHAT PISSES ME OFF??

That we still lack superpowers.

With all the radiation, chemicals, and terrible science experiments that are out there in the world, you'd think SOMEONE would have come down with some sort of superpower by now!

And if there is someone with superpowers out there and you're hiding it from me . . . I'm very annoyed with you right now.

99
YOU KNOW WHAT PISSES ME OFF??

The phrase "pics or it didn't happen."

There aren't pictures of my mother getting cut open and a doctor ripping me out, but it still happened!!!

Why do I have to provide a picture of something awesome I did just because you have trust issues! No! I'm not going to disrupt my life to take a picture just in case you don't believe me. Rude. It's rude that you don't trust me. I don't trust you. Ha! How does that feel!?

100

That we can't control the weather yet.

Not only that, but we can't even predict it properly! We have the ability to travel to Mars, perform heart transplants, and make metal tanks soar through the sky, but we can't make clouds go away? How have we not made a safe chemical thingy that makes it rain? Are we just not thinking of this? Scientists say we caused global warming—is that all we really have the ability to do? Pathetic.

101

YOU KNOW WHAT PISSES ME OFF??

The fact that I'm out of space to write.

Because I'm pissed about so many more things!

Acknowledgments

I need to thank my sister, Colleen Ballinger, for putting me in a position to be able to write this book and for telling me to do so. I am forever grateful for the career she has helped me build.

My mom would kill me if I didn't say something about her. So, hi Mom, hi Dad. Thanks for being amazing parents and supporting me in whatever I do. You two are some awesome humans.

I need to give a special thanks to my best friend, Kelly Six. She helped me so much in writing this book, I honestly don't think I could have done it without her. She helped spark ideas, corrected my terrible grammar, and gave me the motivation I needed to finish this thing. So, thank you, Kelly. Thank you for putting up with the endless text messages, e-mails, phone calls, and Skype sessions. You're the true MVP.